# Handbook of Organized Crime

Editor

Masako Gillette

*Scribbles*

Year of Publication 2018

ISBN : 9789352979837

Book Published by

# Scribbles

*(An Imprint of Alpha Editions)*

email - alphaedis@gmail.com

Produced by: PediaPress GmbH
Limburg an der Lahn
Germany
http://pediapress.com/

The content within this book was generated collaboratively by volunteers. Please be advised that nothing found here has necessarily been reviewed by people with the expertise required to provide you with complete, accurate or reliable information. Some information in this book may be misleading or simply wrong. Alpha Editions and PediaPress does not guarantee the validity of the information found here. If you need specific advice (for example, medical, legal, financial, or risk management) please seek a professional who is licensed or knowledgeable in that area.

Sources, licenses and contributors of the articles and images are listed in the section entitled "References". Parts of the books may be licensed under the GNU Free Documentation License. A copy of this license is included in the section entitled "GNU Free Documentation License"

The views and characters expressed in the book are those of the contributors and his/her imagination and do not represent the views of the Publisher.

# Contents

**Articles**    **1**
    Organized crime . . . . . . . . . . . . . . . . . . . . . . . . . 1

**Appendix**    **31**
    References . . . . . . . . . . . . . . . . . . . . . . . . . . . . 31
    Article Sources and Contributors . . . . . . . . . . . . . . . . . 33
    Image Sources, Licenses and Contributors . . . . . . . . . . . . 34

**Article Licenses**    **35**

**Index**    **37**

# Organized crime

Criminology and penology

- v
- t
- e[1]

**Organized crime** is a category of transnational, national, or local groupings of highly centralized enterprises run by criminals who intend to engage in illegal activity, most commonly for money and profit. Some criminal organizations, such as terrorist groups, are politically motivated. Sometimes criminal organizations force people to do business with them, such as when a gang extorts money from shopkeepers for so-called "protection".[2] Gangs may become disciplined enough to be considered *organized*. A **criminal organization** or gang can also be referred to as a **mafia**, **mob**, or **crime syndicate**; the network, subculture and community of criminals may be referred to as the **underworld**. European sociologists (e.g. Diego Gambetta) define the mafia as a type of organized crime group that specializes in the supply of extra-legal protection and quasi law enforcement. Gambetta's classic work on *the Sicilian Mafia*[3] generates an economic study of the mafia, which exerts great influence on studies of *the Russian Mafia*,[4] *the Chinese Mafia*,[5] *Hong Kong Triads*[6] and *the Japanese Yakuza*.[7]

Other organizations—including states, militaries, police forces, and corporations—may sometimes use organized-crime methods to conduct their activities, but their powers derive from their status as formal social institutions. There is a tendency to distinguish organized crime from other forms of crime, such as white-collar crime, financial crimes, political crimes, war crime, state crimes, and treason. This distinction is not always apparent and academics continue to debate the matter.[8] For example, in failed states that can no longer perform basic functions such as education, security, or governance (usually due to fractious violence or to extreme poverty), organized crime, governance and war sometimes complement each other. The term "Oligarchy" has been usedWikipedia:Manual of Style/Words to watch#Unsupported attributions to describe democratic countries whose political, social and economic institutions come under the control of a few families and business oligarchs.[9]

In the United States, the Organized Crime Control Act (1970) defines organized crime as "[t]he unlawful activities of [...] a highly organized, disciplined association [...]". Criminal activity as a structured process is referred to as racketeering. In the UK, police estimate that organized crime involves up to 38,000 people operating in 6,000 various groups.[10] Due to the escalating violence of Mexico's drug war, a report issued by the United States Department of Justice characterizes the Mexican drug cartels as the "greatest organized crime threat to the United States".

# Models

## Organizational

### Patron-client networks

Patron-client networks are defined by fluid interactions. They produce crime groups that operate as smaller units within the overall network, and as such tend towards valuing significant others, familiarity of social and economic environments, or tradition. These networks are usually composed of:

- Hierarchies based on 'naturally' forming family, social and cultural traditions;
- 'Tight-knit' focus of activity/labor;
- Fraternal or nepotistic value systems;
- Personalized activity; including family rivalries, territorial disputes, recruitment and training of family members, etc.;
- Entrenched belief systems, reliance of tradition (including religion, family values, cultural expectations, class politics, gender roles, etc.); and,
- Communication and rule enforcement mechanisms dependent on organizational structure, social etiquette, history of criminal involvement, and collective decision-making.

## Bureaucratic/corporate operations

Bureaucratic/corporate organized crime groups are defined by the general rigidity of their internal structures. They focus more on how the operations works, succeeds, sustains itself or avoids retribution, they are generally typified by:

- A complex authority structure;
- An extensive division of labor between classes within the organization;
- Meritocratic (as opposed to cultural or social attributes);
- Responsibilities carried out in an impersonal manner;
- Extensive written rules/regulations (as opposed to cultural praxis dictating action); and,
- 'Top-down' communication and rule enforcement mechanisms.

However, this model of operation has some flaws:

- The 'top-down' communication strategy is susceptible to interception, more so further down the hierarchy being communicated to;
- Maintaining written records jeopardizes the security of the organization and relies on increased security measures;
- Infiltration at lower levels in the hierarchy can jeopardize the entire organization (a 'house of cards' effect); and,
- Death, injury, incarceration or internal power struggles dramatically heighten the insecurity of operations.

While bureaucratic operations emphasize business processes and strongly authoritarian hierarchies, these are based on enforcing power relationships rather than an overlying aim of protectionism, sustainability or growth.

## Youth and street gangs

An estimate on youth street gangs nationwide provided by Hannigan, et al., marked an increase of 35% between 2002 and 2010. A distinctive gang culture underpins many, but not all, organized groups; this may develop through recruiting strategies, social learning processes in the corrective system experienced by youth, family or peer involvement in crime, and the coercive actions of criminal authority figures. The term "street gang" is commonly used interchangeably with "youth gang," referring to neighborhood or street-based youth groups that meet "gang" criteria. Miller (1992) defines a street gang as "a self-formed association of peers, united by mutual interests, with identifiable leadership and internal organization, who act collectively or as individuals to achieve specific purposes, including the conduct of illegal activity and control of a particular territory, facility, or enterprise."[11] Some reasons youth join gangs include to feel accepted, attain status, and increase their self-esteem. A

**Figure 1:** *Jamaican gang leader Christopher Coke*

sense of unity brings together many of the youth gangs that lack the family aspect at home.

"Zones of transition" are deteriorating neighborhoods with shifting populations. In such areas, conflict between groups, fighting, "turf wars", and theft promote solidarity and cohesion. Cohen (1955): working class teenagers joined gangs due to frustration of inability to achieve status and goals of the middle class; Cloward and Ohlin (1960): blocked opportunity, but unequal distribution of opportunities lead to creating different types of gangs (that is, some focused on robbery and property theft, some on fighting and conflict and some were retreatists focusing on drug taking); Spergel (1966) was one of the first criminologists to focus on *evidence-based practice* rather than intuition into gang life and culture. Participation in gang-related events during adolescence perpetuate a pattern of maltreatment on their own children years later. Klein (1971) like Spergel studied the effects on members of social workers' interventions. More interventions actually lead to greater gang participation and solidarity and bonds between members. Downes and Rock (1988) on Parker's analysis: strain theory applies, labeling theory (from experience with police and courts), control theory (involvement in trouble from early childhood and the eventual decision that the costs outweigh the benefits) and conflict theories. No ethnic group is more disposed to gang involvement than another, rather it is the status of being marginalized, alienated or rejected that makes some groups more vulnerable to gang formation, and this would also be accounted for in the effect of social exclusion, especially in terms of recruitment and retention. These may also be defined by age (typically youth) or peer group influences, and the permanence or consistency of their criminal activity. These groups also form their own symbolic identity or public representation which are recognizable by the community at large (include colors, symbols, patches, flags and tattoos).

Research has focused on whether the gangs have formal structures, clear hierarchies and leadership in comparison with adult groups, and whether they are rational in pursuit of their goals, though positions on structures, hierarchies and defined roles are conflicting. Some studied street gangs involved in drug dealing - finding that their structure and behavior had a degree of organizational rationality. Members saw themselves as organized criminals; gangs were formal-rational organizations, Strong organizational structures, well defined roles and rules that guided members' behavior. Also a specified and regular means of income (i.e., drugs). Padilla (1992) agreed with the two above. However some have found these to be loose rather than well-defined and lacking persistent focus, there was relatively low cohesion, few shared goals and little organizational structure. Shared norms, value and loyalties were low, structures "chaotic", little role differentiation or clear distribution of labor. Similarly, the use of violence does not conform to the principles behind protection rackets, political intimidation and drug trafficking activities employed by those adult groups. In many cases gang members graduate from youth gangs to highly developed OC groups, with some already in contact with such syndicates and through this we see a greater propensity for imitation. Gangs and traditional criminal organizations cannot be universally linked (Decker, 1998), however there are clear benefits to both the adult and youth organization through their association. In terms of structure, no single crime group is archetypal, though in most cases there are well-defined patterns of vertical integration (where criminal groups attempt to control the supply and demand), as is the case in arms, sex and drug trafficking.

## Individual difference

### Entrepreneurial

The entrepreneurial model looks at either the individual criminal or a smaller group of organized criminals, that capitalize off the more fluid 'group-association' of contemporary organized crime. This model conforms to social learning theory or differential association in that there are clear associations and interaction between criminals where knowledge may be shared, or values enforced, however, it is argued that rational choice is not represented in this. The choice to commit a certain act, or associate with other organized crime groups, may be seen as much more of an entrepreneurial decision - contributing to the continuation of a criminal enterprise, by maximizing those aspects that protect or support their own individual gain. In this context, the role of risk is also easily understandable, however it is debatable whether the underlying motivation should be seen as true entrepreneurship or entrepreneurship as a product of some social disadvantage.

The criminal organization, much in the same way as one would assess pleasure and pain, weighs such factors as legal, social and economic risk to determine potential profit and loss from certain criminal activities. This decision-making process rises from the entrepreneurial efforts of the group's members, their motivations and the environments in which they work. Opportunism is also a key factor – the organized criminal or criminal group is likely to frequently reorder the criminal associations they maintain, the types of crimes they perpetrate, and how they function in the public arena (recruitment, reputation, etc.) in order to ensure efficiency, capitalization and protection of their interests.

## Multimodel approach

Culture and ethnicity provide an environment where trust and communication between criminals can be efficient and secure. This may ultimately lead to a competitive advantage for some groups; however, it is inaccurate to adopt this as the only determinant of classification in organized crime. This categorization includes the Sicilian Mafia, Jamaican posses, Colombian drug trafficking groups, Nigerian organized crime groups, Corsican mafia, Japanese Yakuza (or Boryokudan), Korean criminal groups and ethnic Chinese criminal groups. From this perspective, organized crime is not a modern phenomenon - the construction of 17th and 18th century crime gangs fulfill all the present day criteria of criminal organizations (in opposition to the Alien Conspiracy Theory). These roamed the rural borderlands of central Europe embarking on many of the same illegal activities associated with today's crime organizations, with the exception of money laundering. When the French revolution created strong nation states, the criminal gangs moved to other poorly controlled regions like the Balkans and Southern Italy, where the seeds were sown for the Sicilian Mafia - the lynchpin of organized crime in the New World.

| Model type | Environment | Group | Processes | Impacts |
|---|---|---|---|---|
| National | Historical or cultural basis | Family or hierarchy | Secrecy/- bonds. Links to insurgents | Local corruption/- influence. Fearful community. |
| Transnational | Politically and economically unstable | Vertical integration | Legitimate cover | Stable supply of illicit goods. High-level corruption. |

| Transnational/-transactional | Any | Flexible. Small size. | Violent. Opportunistic. Risk taking | Unstable supply of range of illicit goods. Exploits young local offenders. |
|---|---|---|---|---|
| Entrepreneurial/-transactional | Developed/-high technology regions | Individuals or pairs. | Operating through legitimate enterprise | Provision of illicit services, e.g., money laundering, fraud, criminal networks. |

## Typical activities

Organized crime groups provide a range of illegal services and goods. Organized crime often victimizes businesses through the use of extortion or theft and fraud activities like hijacking cargo trucks, robbing goods, committing bankruptcy fraud (also known as "bust-out"), insurance fraud or stock fraud (inside trading). Organized crime groups also victimize individuals by car theft (either for dismantling at "chop shops" or for export), art theft, bank robbery, burglary, jewelry and gems theft and heists, shoplifting, computer hacking, credit card fraud, economic espionage, embezzlement, identity theft, and securities fraud ("pump and dump" scam). Some organized crime groups defraud national, state, or local governments by bid rigging public projects, counterfeiting money, smuggling or manufacturing untaxed alcohol (bootlegging) or cigarettes (buttlegging), and providing immigrant workers to avoid taxes.

Organized crime groups seek out corrupt public officials in executive, law enforcement, and judicial roles so that their activities can avoid, or at least receive early warnings about, investigation and prosecution.

Activities of organized crime include loansharking of money at very high interest rates, assassination, blackmailing, bombings, bookmaking and illegal gambling, confidence tricks, copyright infringement, counterfeiting of intellectual property, fencing, kidnapping, prostitution, smuggling, drug trafficking, arms trafficking, oil smuggling, antiquities smuggling, organ trafficking, contract killing, identity document forgery, money laundering, bribery, seduction, electoral fraud, insurance fraud, point shaving, price fixing, illegal taxicab operation, illegal dumping of toxic waste, illegal trading of nuclear materials, military equipment smuggling, nuclear weapons smuggling, passport fraud, providing illegal immigration and cheap labor, people smuggling, trading in endangered species, and trafficking in human beings. Organized crime groups also do a range of business and labor racketeering activities, such as skimming casinos, insider trading, setting up monopolies in industries such as garbage collecting, construction and cement pouring, bid rigging, getting "no-show" and "no-work" jobs, political corruption and bullying.

## Violence

### Assault

The commission of violent crime may form part of a criminal organization's 'tools' used to achieve criminogenic goals (for example, its threatening, authoritative, coercive, terror-inducing, or rebellious role), due to psychosocial factors (cultural conflict, aggression, rebellion against authority, access to illicit substances, counter-cultural dynamic), or may, in and of itself, be crime rationally chosen by individual criminals and the groups they form. Assaults are used for coercive measures, to "rough up" debtors, competition or recruits, in the commission of robberies, in connection to other property offenses, and as an expression of counter-cultural authority; violence is normalized within criminal organizations (in direct opposition to mainstream society) and the locations they control. Whilst the intensity of violence is dependent on the types of crime the organization is involved in (as well as their organizational structure or cultural tradition) aggressive acts range on a spectrum from low-grade physical assaults to murder. Bodily harm and grievous bodily harm, within the context of organized crime, must be understood as indicators of intense social and cultural conflict, motivations contrary to the security of the public, and other psychosocial factors.

### Murder

Murder has evolved from the honor and vengeance killings of the Yakuza or Sicilian mafia which placed large physical and symbolic importance on the act of murder, its purposes and consequences, to a much less discriminate form of expressing power, enforcing criminal authority, achieving retribution or eliminating competition. The role of the hit man has been generally consistent throughout the history of organized crime, whether that be due to the efficiency or expediency of hiring a professional assassin or the need to distance oneself from the commission of murderous acts (making it harder to prove liability). This may include the assassination of notable figures (public, private or criminal), once again dependent on authority, retribution or competition. Revenge killings, armed robberies, violent disputes over controlled territories and offenses against members of the public must also be considered when looking at the dynamic between different criminal organizations and their (at times) conflicting needs.

## Terrorism

In addition to what is considered traditional organized crime involving direct crimes of fraud swindles, scams, racketeering and other Racketeer Influenced and Corrupt Organizations Act (RICO) predicate acts motivated for the accumulation of monetary gain, there is also non-traditional organized crime which is engaged in for political or ideological gain or acceptance. Such crime groups are often labelled terrorist groups.

There is no universally agreed, legally binding, criminal law definition of terrorism.[12,13] Common definitions of **terrorism** refer only to those violent acts which are intended to create fear (terror), are perpetrated for a religious, political or ideological goal, deliberately target or disregard the safety of non-combatants (e.g., neutral military personnel or civilians), and are committed by non-government agencies.Wikipedia:Citation needed Some definitions also include acts of unlawful violence and war, especially crimes against humanity (*see the Nuremberg Trials*), Allied authorities deeming the German Nazi Party, its paramilitary and police organizations, and numerous associations subsidiary to the Nazi Party "criminal organizations". The use of similar tactics by criminal organizations for protection rackets or to enforce a code of silence is usually not labeled terrorism though these same actions may be labeled terrorism when done by a politically motivated group.

Notable groups include Al-Qaeda, Animal Liberation Front, Army of God, Black Liberation Army, The Covenant, The Sword, and the Arm of the Lord, Earth Liberation Front, Irish Republican Army, Kurdistan Workers' Party, Lashkar e Toiba, May 19th Communist Organization, The Order, Revolutionary Armed Forces of Colombia, Symbionese Liberation Army, Taliban, United Freedom Front and Weather Underground.Wikipedia:Citation needed.

## Other

- Arms trafficking
- Arson
- Coercion
- Extortion
- Protection racket
- Sexual assault

## Financial crime

Organized crime groups generate large amounts of money by activities such as drug trafficking, arms smuggling and financial crime.[14] This is of little use to them unless they can disguise it and convert it into funds that are available for investment into legitimate enterprise. The methods they use for converting its 'dirty' money into 'clean' assets encourages corruption. Organized crime groups need to hide the money's illegal origin. It allows for the expansion of OC groups, as the 'laundry' or 'wash cycle' operates to cover the money trail and convert proceeds of crime into usable assets. Money laundering is bad for international and domestic trade, banking reputations and for effective governments and rule of law. Accurate figures for the amounts of criminal proceeds laundered are almost impossible to calculate, and the Financial Action Task Force on Money Laundering (FATF), an intergovernmental body set up to combat money laundering, has stated that "overall it is absolutely impossible to produce a reliable estimate of the amount of money laundered and therefore the FATF does not publish any figures in this regard". However, in the US estimated figures of money laundering have been put at between $200 – $600 billion per year throughout the 1990s (US Congress Office 1995; Robinson 1996), and in 2002 this was estimated between $500 billion to $1 trillion per year (UN 2002). This would make organized crime the third largest business in world after foreign exchange and oil (Robinson 1996). The rapid growth of money laundering is due to:

- the scale of organized crime precluding it from being a cash business - groups have little option but to convert its proceeds into legitimate funds and do so by investment, by developing legitimate businesses and purchasing property;
- globalization of communications and commerce - technology has made rapid transfer of funds across international borders much easier, with groups continuously changing techniques to avoid investigation; and,
- a lack of effective financial regulation in parts of the global economy.

Money laundering is a three-stage process:

- Placement: (also called immersion) groups 'smurf' small amounts at a time to avoid suspicion; physical disposal of money by moving crime funds into the legitimate financial system; may involve bank complicity, mixing licit and illicit funds, cash purchases and smuggling currency to safe havens.
- Layering: disguises the trail to foil pursuit. Also called 'heavy soaping'. It involves creating false paper trails, converting cash into assets by cash purchases.
- Integration: (also called 'spin dry'): Making it into clean taxable income by real-estate transactions, sham loans, foreign bank complicity and false import and export transactions.

Means of money laundering:

- Money transmitters, black money markets purchasing goods, gambling, increasing the complexity of the money trail.

- Underground banking (flying money), involves clandestine 'bankers' around the world.
- It often involves otherwise legitimate banks and professionals.

The policy aim in this area is to make the financial markets transparent, and minimize the circulation of criminal money and its cost upon legitimate markets.

## Counterfeiting

In 2007, the OECD reported the scope of counterfeit products to include food, pharmaceuticals, pesticides, electrical components, tobacco and even household cleaning products in addition to the usual films, music, literature, games and other electrical appliances, software and fashion. A number of qualitative changes in the trade of counterfeit products:

- a large increase in fake goods which are dangerous to health and safety;
- most products repossessed by authorities are now household items rather than luxury goods;
- a growing number of technological products; and,
- production is now operated on an industrial scale.

## Tax evasion

The economic effects of organized crime have been approached from a number of both theoretical and empirical positions, however the nature of such activity allows for misrepresentation. The level of taxation taken by a nation-state, rates of unemployment, mean household incomes and level of satisfaction with government and other economic factors all contribute to the likelihood of criminals to participate in tax evasion. As most organized crime is perpetrated in the liminal state between legitimate and illegitimate markets, these economic factors must adjusted to ensure the optimal amount of taxation without promoting the practice of tax evasion. As with any other crime, technological advancements have made the commission of tax evasion easier, faster and more globalized. The ability for organized criminals to operate fraudulent financial accounts, utilize illicit offshore bank accounts, access tax havens or tax shelters, and operating goods smuggling syndicates to evade importation taxes help ensure financial sustainability, security from law enforcement, general anonymity and the continuation of their operations.

# Cybercrime

### Internet fraud

**Identity theft** is a form of fraud or cheating of another person's identity in which someone pretends to be someone else by assuming that person's identity, typically in order to access resources or obtain credit and other benefits in that person's name. Victims of identity theft (those whose identity has been assumed by the identity thief) can suffer adverse consequences if held accountable for the perpetrator's actions, as can organizations and individuals who are defrauded by the identity thief, and to that extent are also victims. **Internet fraud** refers to the actual use of Internet services to present fraudulent solicitations to prospective victims, to conduct fraudulent transactions, or to transmit the proceeds of fraud to financial institutions or to others connected with the scheme. In the context of organized crime, both may serve as means through which other criminal activity may be successfully perpetrated or as the primary goal themselves. Email fraud, advance-fee fraud, romance scams, employment scams, and other phishing scams are the most common and most widely used forms of identity theft, though with the advent of social networking fake websites, accounts and other fraudulent or deceitful activity has become commonplace.

### Copyright infringement

Copyright infringement is the unauthorized or prohibited use of works under copyright, infringing the copyright holder's exclusive rights, such as the right to reproduce or perform the copyrighted work, or to make derivative works. Whilst almost universally considered under civil procedure, the impact and intent of organized criminal operations in this area of crime has been the subject of much debate. Article 61 of the Agreement on Trade-Related Aspects of Intellectual Property Rights (TRIPs) requires that signatory countries establish criminal procedures and penalties in cases of willful trademark counterfeiting or copyright piracy on a commercial scale. More recently copyright holders have demanded that states provide criminal sanctions for all types of copyright infringement. Organized criminal groups capitalize on consumer complicity, advancements in security and anonymity technology, emerging markets and new methods of product transmission, and the consistent nature of these provides a stable financial basis for other areas of organized crime.Wikipedia:Citation needed

## Cyberwarfare

**Cyberwarfare** refers to politically motivated hacking to conduct sabotage and espionage. It is a form of information warfare sometimes seen as analogous to conventional warfare although this analogy is controversial for both its accuracy and its political motivation. It has been defined as activities by a nation-state to penetrate another nation's computers or networks with the intention of causing civil damage or disruption.[15] Moreover, it acts as the "fifth domain of warfare,"[16] and William J. Lynn, U.S. Deputy Secretary of Defense, states that "as a doctrinal matter, the Pentagon has formally recognized cyberspace as a new domain in warfare . . . [which] has become just as critical to military operations as land, sea, air, and space."[17] Cyber espionage is the practice of obtaining confidential, sensitive, proprietary or classified information from individuals, competitors, groups, or governments using illegal exploitation methods on internet, networks, software and/or computers. There is also a clear military, political, or economic motivation. Unsecured information may be intercepted and modified, making espionage possible internationally. The recently established Cyber Command is currently debating whether such activities as commercial espionage or theft of intellectual property are criminal activities or actual "breaches of national security." Furthermore, military activities that use computers and satellites for coordination are at risk of equipment disruption. Orders and communications can be intercepted or replaced. Power, water, fuel, communications, and transportation infrastructure all may be vulnerable to sabotage. According to Clarke, the civilian realm is also at risk, noting that the security breaches have already gone beyond stolen credit card numbers, and that potential targets can also include the electric power grid, trains, or the stock market.[18]

## Computer viruses

The term "computer virus" may be used as an overarching phrase to include all types of true viruses, malware, including computer worms, Trojan horses, most rootkits, spyware, dishonest adware and other malicious and unwanted software (though all are technically unique), and proves to be quite financially lucrative for criminal organizations, offering greater opportunities for fraud and extortion whilst increasing security, secrecy and anonymity. Worms may be utilized by organized crime groups to exploit security vulnerabilities (duplicating itself automatically across other computers a given network), while a Trojan horse is a program that appears harmless but hides malicious functions (such as retrieval of stored confidential data, corruption of information, or interception of transmissions). Worms and Trojan horses, like viruses, may harm a computer system's data or performance. Applying the Internet model of organized crime, the proliferation of computer viruses and other malicious software promotes a sense of detachment between the perpetrator (whether that be the criminal organization or another individual) and the victim; this may help to explain vast increases in cyber-crime such as these for the purpose of ideological crime or terrorism. In mid July 2010, security experts discovered a malicious software program that had infiltrated factory computers and had spread to plants around the world. It is considered "the first attack on critical industrial infrastructure that sits at the foundation of modern economies," notes the *New York Times*.[19]

## White-collar crime and corruption

### Corporate crime

Corporate crime refers to crimes committed either by a corporation (i.e., a business entity having a separate legal personality from the natural persons that manage its activities), or by individuals that may be identified with a corporation or other business entity (see vicarious liability and corporate liability). Note that some forms of corporate corruption may not actually be criminal if they are not specifically illegal under a given system of laws. For example, some jurisdictions allow insider trading.

### Labor racketeering

Labor racketeering has developed since the 1930s, affecting national and international construction, mining, energy production and transportation sectors immensely. Activity has focused on the importation of cheap or unfree labor, involvement with union and public officials (political corruption), and counterfeiting.

### Political corruption

Political corruption is the use of legislated powers by government officials for illegitimate private gain. Misuse of government power for other purposes, such as repression of political opponents and general police brutality, is not considered political corruption. Neither are illegal acts by private persons or corporations not directly involved with the government. An illegal act by an officeholder constitutes political corruption only if the act is directly related to their official duties. Forms of corruption vary, but include bribery, extortion, cronyism, nepotism, patronage, graft, and embezzlement. While corruption may facilitate criminal enterprise such as drug trafficking, money laundering, and human trafficking, it is not restricted to these activities. The activities that constitute illegal corruption differ depending on the country or jurisdiction. For instance, certain political funding practices that are legal in one place may be illegal in another. In some cases, government officials have broad or poorly defined powers, which make it difficult to distinguish between legal and illegal actions. Worldwide, bribery alone is estimated to involve over 1 trillion US

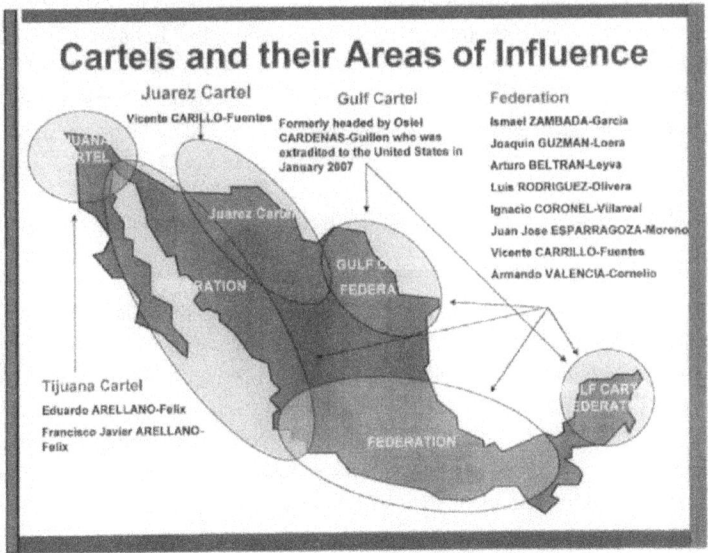

**Figure 2:** *Mexican drug cartels and their areas of influence*

dollars annually.[20] A state of unrestrained political corruption is known as a kleptocracy, literally meaning "rule by thieves".

## Drug trafficking

Heroin: Source countries / production: three major regions known as the Golden Triangle (Burma, Laos, Thailand), Golden Crescent (Afghanistan) and Central and South America. There are suggestions that due to the continuing decline in opium production in South East Asia, traffickers may begin to look to Afghanistan as a source of heroin."

## Human trafficking

### Sex trafficking

Human trafficking for the purpose of sexual exploitation is a major cause of contemporary sexual slavery and is primarily for prostituting women and children into sex industries. Sexual slavery encompasses most, if not all, forms of forced prostitution.[21] The terms "forced prostitution" or "enforced prostitution" appear in international and humanitarian conventions but have been insufficiently understood and inconsistently applied. "Forced prostitution" generally refers to conditions of control over a person who is coerced by another to engage in sexual activity. Official numbers of individuals in sexual slavery worldwide vary. In 2001 International Organization for Migration estimated 400,000, the Federal Bureau of Investigation estimated 700,000 and UNICEF estimated 1.75 million.[22] The most common destinations for victims of human trafficking are Thailand, Japan, Israel, Belgium, the Netherlands, Germany, Italy, Turkey and the United States, according to a report by UNODC.

### Illegal immigration and people smuggling

*See Snakehead (gang), Coyotaje*

**People smuggling** is defined as "the facilitation, transportation, attempted transportation or illegal entry of a person or persons across an international border, in violation of one or more countries laws, either clandestinely or through deception, such as the use of fraudulent documents". The term is understood as and often used interchangeably with migrant smuggling, which is defined by the United Nations Convention Against Transnational Organized Crime as "...the procurement, in order to obtain, directly or indirectly, a financial or other material benefit, of the illegal entry of a person into a state party of which the person is not a national". This practice has increased over the past few decades and today now accounts for a significant portion of illegal immigration in countries around the world. People smuggling generally takes place with the consent of the person or persons being smuggled, and common reasons for individuals seeking to be smuggled include employment and economic opportunity, personal and/or familial betterment, and escape from persecution or conflict.

### Contemporary slavery and forced labor

The number of slaves today remains as high as 12 million to 27 million. This is probably the smallest proportion of slaves to the rest of the world's population in history. Most are debt slaves, largely in South Asia, who are under debt bondage incurred by lenders, sometimes even for generations. It is the fastest growing criminal industry and is predicted to eventually outgrow drug trafficking.

# Historical origins

## Pre-nineteenth century

Today, crime is sometimes thought of as an urban phenomenon, but for most of human history it was the rural interfaces that encountered the majority of crimes (bearing in mind the fact that for most of human history, rural areas were the vast majority of inhabited places). For the most part, within a village, members kept crime at very low rates; however, outsiders such as pirates, highwaymen, and bandits attacked trade routes and roads, at times severely disrupting commerce, raising costs, insurance rates and prices to the consumer. According to criminologist Paul Lunde, "Piracy and banditry were to the preindustrial world what organized crime is to modern society."[23] <templatestyles src="Template:Quote/styles.css"/>

> If we take a global rather than strictly domestic view, it becomes evident even crime of the organized kind has a long if not necessarily noble heritage. The word 'thug' dates to early 13th-century India, when Thugs, or gangs of criminals, roamed from town to town, looting and pillaging. Smuggling and drug-trafficking rings are as old as the hills in Asia and Africa, and extant criminal organizations in Italy and Japan trace their histories back several centuries...[24]

As Lunde states, "Barbarian conquerors, whether Vandals, Goths, the Norse, Turks or Mongols are not normally thought of as organized crime groups, yet they share many features associated with thriving criminal organizations. They were for the most part non-ideological, predominantly ethnically based, used violence and intimidation, and adhered to their own codes of law." Terrorism is linked to organized crime, but has political aims rather than solely financial ones, so there is overlap but separation between terrorism and organized crime.

## Nineteenth century

During the Victorian era, criminals and gangs started to form organizations which would be collectively become London's criminal underworld. Criminal societies in the underworld started to develop their own ranks and groups which were sometimes called *families*, and were often made up of lower-classes and operated on pick-pocketry, prostitution, forgery and counterfeiting, commercial burglary and even money-laundering schemes. Unique also were the use of slangs and argots used by Victorian criminal societies to distinguish each other. One of the most infamous crime bosses in the Victorian underworld was Adam Worth, who was nicknamed "the Napoleon of the criminal world" or "the Napoleon of Crime" and became the inspiration behind the popular character of Professor Moriarty.[25]

**Figure 3:** *Tattooed Yakuza gangsters*

Organized crime in the United States first came to prominence in the Old West and historians such as Brian J. Robb and Erin H. Turner traced the first organized crime syndicates to the Coschise Cowboy Gang and the Wild Bunch.[26,27] The Cochise Cowboys, though loosely organized, were unique for their criminal operations in the Mexican border, in which they would steal and sell cattle as well smuggled contraband goods in between the countries.[28]

## Twentieth century

Donald Cressey's Cosa Nostra model studied Mafia families exclusively and this limits his broader findings. Structures are formal and rational with allocated tasks, limits on entrance, and influence the rules established for organizational maintenance and sustainability. In this context there is a difference between organized and professional crime; there is well-defined hierarchy of roles for leaders and members, underlying rules and specific goals that determine their behavior, and these are formed as a social system, one that was rationally designed to maximize profits and to provide forbidden goods. Albini saw organized criminal behavior as consisting of networks of patrons and clients, rather than rational hierarchies or secret societies.

The networks are characterized by a loose system of power relations. Each participant is interested in furthering his own welfare. Criminal entrepreneurs are the patrons and they exchange information with their clients in order to obtain their support. Clients include members of gangs, local and national politicians, government officials and people engaged in legitimate business. People in the network may not directly be part of the core criminal organization. Furthering the approach of both Cressey and Albini, Ianni and Ianni studied Italian-American crime syndicates in New York and other cities.

Kinship is seen as the basis of organized crime rather than the structures Cressey had identified; this includes fictive godparental and affinitive ties as well as those based on blood relations, and it is the impersonal actions, not the status or affiliations of their members, that define the group. Rules of conduct and behavioral aspects of power and networks and roles include the following:

- family operates as a social unit, with social and business functions merged;
- leadership positions down to middle management are kinship based;
- the higher the position, the closer the kinship relationship;
- group assigns leadership positions to a central group of family members, including fictive godparental relationship reinforcement;
- the leadership group are assigned to legal or illegal enterprises, but not both; and,
- transfer of money, from legal and illegal business, and back to illegal business is by individuals, not companies.

Strong family ties are derived from the traditions of southern Italy, where family rather than the church or state is the basis of social order and morality.

### The "disorganized crime" and choice theses

One of the most important trends to emerge in criminological thinking about OC in recent years is the suggestion that it is not, in a formal sense, "organized" at all. Evidence includes lack of centralized control, absence of formal lines of communication, fragmented organizational structure. It is distinctively disorganized. For example, Seattle's crime network in the 1970s and 80s consisted of groups of businessmen, politicians and of law enforcement officers. They all had links to a national network via Meyer Lansky, who was powerful, but there was no evidence that Lansky or anyone else exercised centralized control over them.

While some crime involved well-known criminal hierarchies in the city, criminal activity was not subject to central management by these hierarchies nor by other controlling groups, nor were activities limited to a finite number of objectives. The networks of criminals involved with the crimes did not exhibit organizational cohesion. Too much emphasis had been placed on the Mafia as controlling OC. The Mafia were certainly powerful but they "were part of a heterogeneous underworld, a network characterized by complex webs of relationships." OC groups were violent and aimed at making money but because of the lack of structure and fragmentation of objectives, they were "disorganized".

Further studies showed neither bureaucracy nor kinship groups are the primary structure of organized crime, rather they were in partnerships or a series of joint business ventures. Despite these conclusions, all researchers observed a degree of managerial activities among the groups they studied. All observed networks and a degree of persistence, and there may be utility in focusing on the identification of organizing roles of people and events rather than the group's structure. There may be three main approaches to understand the organizations in terms of their roles as social systems:

- organizations as rational systems: Highly formalized structures in terms of bureaucracy's and hierarchy, with formal systems of rules regarding authority and highly specific goals;
- organizations as natural systems: Participants may regard the organization as an end in itself, not merely a means to some other end. Promoting group values to maintain solidarity is high on the agenda. They do not rely on profit maximization. Their perversity and violence in respect of relationships is often remarkable, but they are characterized by their focus on the connections between their members, their associates and their victims; and,
- organizations open systems: High levels of interdependence between themselves and the environment in which they operate. There is no one way in which they are organized or how they operate. They are adaptable and change to meet the demands of their changing environments and circumstances.

Organized crime groups may be a combination of all three.

**International governance approach**

International consensus on defining organized crime has become important since the 1970s due its increased prevalence and impact. e.g., UN in 1976 and EU 1998. OC is "...the large scale and complex criminal activity carried on by groups of persons, however loosely or tightly organized for the enrichment of those participating at the expense of the community and its members. It is frequently accomplished through ruthless disregard of any law, including offenses against the person and frequently in connection with political corruption." (UN) "A criminal organization shall mean a lasting, structured association of two or more persons, acting in concert with a view to committing crimes or other offenses which are punishable by deprivation of liberty or a detention order of a maximum of at least four years or a more serious penalty, whether such crimes or offenses are an end in themselves or a means of obtaining material benefits and, if necessary, of improperly influencing the operation of public authorities." (UE) Not all groups exhibit the same characteristics of structure. However, violence and corruption and the pursuit of multiple enterprises and continuity serve to form the essence of OC activity.

There are eleven characteristics from the European Commission and Europol pertinent to a working definition of organized crime. Six of those must be satisfied and the four in italics are mandatory. Summarized, they are:

- *more than two people*;
- their own appointed tasks;
- activity over a *prolonged or indefinite period of time*;
- the use discipline or control;
- perpetration of *serious criminal offenses*;
- operations on an international or transnational level;
- the use violence or other intimidation;
- the use of commercial or businesslike structures;
- engagement in money laundering;
- exertion of influence on politics, media, public administration, judicial authorities or the economy; and,
- *motivated by the pursuit of profit and/or power,*

with the Convention against Transnational Organized Crime (the *Palermo Convention*) having a similar definition:

- organized criminal: structured group, three or more people, one or more serious crimes, in order to obtain financial or other material benefit;
- serious crime: offense punishable by at least four years in prison; and,
- structured group: Not randomly formed but doesn't need formal structure,

Others stress the importance of power, profit and perpetuity, defining organized criminal behavior as:

- nonideological: i.e., profit driven;
- hierarchical: few elites and many operatives;
- limited or exclusive membership: maintain secrecy and loyalty of members;
- perpetuating itself: Recruitment process and policy;
- willing to use illegal violence and bribery;
- specialized division of labor: to achieve organization goal;
- monopolistic: Market control to maximize profits; and,
- has explicit rules and regulations: Codes of honor.

Definitions need to bring together its legal and social elements. OC has widespread social, political and economic effects. It uses violence and corruption to achieve its ends: "OC when group primarily focused on illegal profits

systematically commit crimes that adversely affect society and are capable of successfully shielding their activities, in particular by being willing to use physical violence or eliminate individuals by way of corruption."
It is a mistake to use the term "OC" as though it denotes a clear and well-defined phenomenon. The evidence regarding OC "shows a less well-organized, very diversified landscape of organizing criminals...the economic activities of these organizing criminals can be better described from the viewpoint of 'crime enterprises' than from a conceptually unclear frameworks such as 'OC'." Many of the definitions emphasize the 'group nature' of OC, the 'organization' of its members, its use of violence or corruption to achieve its goals, and its extra-jurisdictional character....OC may appear in many forms at different times and in different places. Due to the variety of definitions, there is "evident danger" in asking "what is OC?" and expecting a simple answer.

**The locus of power and organized crime**

Some espouse that all organized crime operates at an international level, though there is currently no international court capable of trying offenses resulting from such activities (the International Criminal Court's remit extends only to dealing with people accused of offenses against humanity, e.g., genocide). If a network operates primarily from one jurisdiction and carries out its illicit operations there and in some other jurisdictions it is 'international,' though it may be appropriate to use the term 'transnational' only to label the activities of a major crime group that is centered in no one jurisdiction but operating in many. The understanding of organized crime has therefore progressed to combined internationalization and an understanding of social conflict into one of power, control, efficiency risk and utility, all within the context of organizational theory. The accumulation of social, economic and political power have sustained themselves as a core concerns of all criminal organizations:

- social: criminal groups seek to develop social control in relation to particular communities;
- economic: seek to exert influence by means of corruption and by coercion of legitimate and illegitimate praxis; and,
- political: criminal groups use corruption and violence to attain power and status.

Contemporary organized crime may be very different from traditional Mafia style, particularly in terms of the distribution and centralization of power, authority structures and the concept of 'control' over one's territory and organization. There is a tendency away from centralization of power and reliance upon family ties towards a fragmentation of structures and informality of relationships in crime groups. Organized crime most typically flourishes when a central government and civil society is disorganized, weak, absent or untrusted. This may occur in a society facing periods of political, economic or social turmoil or transition, such as a change of government or a period of rapid economic development, particularly if the society lacks strong and established institutions and the rule of law. The dissolution of the Soviet Union and the Revolutions of 1989 in Eastern Europe that saw the downfall of the Communist Bloc created a breeding ground for criminal organizations.

The newest growth sectors for organized crime are identity theft and online extortion. These activities are troubling because they discourage consumers from using the Internet for e-commerce. E-commerce was supposed to level the playing ground between small and large businesses, but the growth of online organized crime is leading to the opposite effect; large businesses are able to afford more bandwidth (to resist denial-of-service attacks) and superior security. Furthermore, organized crime using the Internet is much harder to trace down for the police (even though they increasingly deploy cybercops) since most police forces and law enforcement agencies operate within a local or national jurisdiction while the Internet makes it easier for criminal organizations to operate across such boundaries without detection.

In the past criminal organizations have naturally limited themselves by their need to expand, putting them in competition with each other. This competition, often leading to violence, uses valuable resources such as manpower (either killed or sent to prison), equipment and finances. In the United States, James "Whitey" Bulger, the Irish Mob boss of the Winter Hill Gang in Boston turned informant for the Federal Bureau of Investigation (FBI). He used this position to eliminate competition and consolidate power within the city of Boston which led to the imprisonment of several senior organized crime figures including Gennaro Angiulo, underboss of the Patriarca crime family. Infighting sometimes occurs within an organization, such as the Castellamarese war of 1930–31 and the Boston Irish Mob Wars of the 1960s and 1970s.

Today criminal organizations are increasingly working together, realizing that it is better to work in cooperation rather than in competition with each other (once again, consolidating power). This has led to the rise of global criminal organizations such as Mara Salvatrucha, 18th Street gang, and Barrio Azteca. The American Mafia, in addition to having links with organized crime groups in Italy such as the Camorra, the 'Ndrangheta, Sacra Corona Unita, and Sicilian Mafia, has at various times done business with the Irish Mob, Jewish-American organized crime, the Japanese Yakuza, Indian Mafia, the Russian Mafia, Thief in law, and Post-Soviet Organized crime groups, the Chinese Triads, Chinese Tongs, and Asian street gangs, Motorcycle Gangs, and numerous White, Black, and Hispanic prison and street gangs. The United Nations Office on Drugs and Crime estimated that organized crime groups held $322 billion in assets in 2005.

This rise in cooperation between criminal organizations has meant that law enforcement agencies are increasingly having to work together. The FBI operates an organized crime section from its headquarters in Washington, D.C. and is known to work with other national (e.g., Polizia di Stato, Russian Federal Security Service (FSB), and the Royal Canadian Mounted Police), federal (e.g., Bureau of Alcohol, Tobacco, Firearms, and Explosives, Drug Enforcement Administration, United States Marshals Service, Immigration and Customs Enforcement, United States Secret Service, US Diplomatic Security Service, United States Postal Inspection Service, U.S. Customs and Border Protection, United States Border Patrol, and the United States Coast Guard), state (e.g., Massachusetts State Police Special Investigation Unit, New Jersey State Police organized crime unit, Pennsylvania State Police organized crime unit, and the New York State Police Bureau of Criminal Investigation) and city (e.g., New York City Police Department Organized Crime Unit, Philadelphia Police Department Organized crime unit, Chicago Police Organized Crime Unit, and the Los Angeles Police Department Special Operations Division) law enforcement agencies.

# Theoretical background

## Criminal psychology

### Rational choice

This theory treats all individuals as rational operators, committing criminal acts after consideration of all associated risks (detection and punishment) compared with the rewards of crimes (personal, financial etc.). Little emphasis is placed on the offenders' emotional state. The role of criminal organizations in lowering the perceptions of risk and increasing the likelihood of personal benefit is prioritized by this approach, with the organizations structure, purpose, and activity being indicative of the rational choices made by criminals and their organizers.

### Deterrence

This theory sees criminal behavior as reflective of an individual, internal calculation by the criminal that the benefits associated with offending (whether financial or otherwise) outweigh the perceived risks. The perceived strength, importance or infallibility of the criminal organization is directly proportional to the types of crime committed, their intensity and arguably the level of community response. The benefits of participating in organized crime (higher financial rewards, greater socioeconomic control and influence, protection of the family or significant others, perceived freedoms from 'oppressive' laws or norms) contribute greatly to the psychology behind highly organized group offending.

**Social learning**

Criminals learn through associations with one another. The success of organized crime groups is therefore dependent upon the strength of their communication and the enforcement of their value systems, the recruitment and training processes employed to sustain, build or fill gaps in criminal operations. An understanding of this theory sees close associations between criminals, imitation of superiors, and understanding of value systems, processes and authority as the main drivers behind organized crime. Interpersonal relationships define the motivations the individual develops, with the effect of family or peer criminal activity being a strong predictor of inter-generational offending. This theory also developed to include the strengths and weaknesses of reinforcement, which in the context of continuing criminal enterprises may be used to help understand propensities for certain crimes or victims, level of integration into the mainstream culture and likelihood of recidivism / success in rehabilitation.

**Enterprise**

Under this theory, organized crime exists because legitimate markets leave many customers and potential customers unsatisfied. High demand for a particular good or service (e.g., drugs, prostitution, arms, slaves), low levels of risk detection and high profits lead to a conducive environment for entrepreneurial criminal groups to enter the market and profit by supplying those goods and services. For success, there must be:
- an identified market; and,
- a certain rate of consumption (demand) to maintain profit and outweigh perceived risks.

Under these conditions competition is discouraged, ensuring criminal monopolies sustain profits. Legal substitution of goods or services may (by increasing competition) force the dynamic of organized criminal operations to adjust, as will deterrence measures (reducing demand), and the restriction of resources (controlling the ability to supply or produce to supply).

### Differential association

Sutherland goes further to say that deviancy is contingent on conflicting groups within society, and that such groups struggle over the means to define what is criminal or deviant within society. Criminal organizations therefore gravitate around illegal avenues of production, profit-making, protectionism or social control and attempt (by increasing their operations or membership) to make these acceptable. This also explains the propensity of criminal organizations to develop protection rackets, to coerce through the use of violence, aggression and threatening behavior (at times termed 'terrorism'). Preoccupation with methods of accumulating profit highlight the lack of legitimate means to achieve economic or social advantage, as does the organization of white-collar crime or political corruption (though it is debatable whether these are based on wealth, power or both). The ability to effect social norms and practices through political and economic influence (and the enforcement or normalisation of criminogenic needs) may be defined by differential association theory.

## Critical criminology and sociology

### Social disorganization

Social disorganization theory is intended to be applied to neighborhood level street crime, thus the context of gang activity, loosely formed criminal associations or networks, socioeconomic demographic impacts, legitimate access to public resources, employment or education, and mobility give it relevance to organized crime. Where the upper- and lower-classes live in close proximity this can result in feelings of anger, hostility, social injustice and frustration. Criminals experience poverty; and witness affluence they are deprived of and which is virtually impossible for them to attain through conventional means. The concept of neighborhood is central to this theory, as it defines the social learning, locus of control, cultural influences and access to social opportunity experienced by criminals and the groups they form. Fear of or lack of trust in mainstream authority may also be a key contributor to social disorganization; organized crime groups replicate such figures and thus ensure control over the counter-culture. This theory has tended to view violent or anti-social behavior by gangs as reflective of their social disorganization rather than as a product or tool of their organization.

### Anomie

Sociologist Robert K. Merton believed deviance depended on society's definition of success, and the desires of individuals to achieve success through socially defined avenues. Criminality becomes attractive when expectations of being able to fulfill goals (therefore achieving success) by legitimate means

## By nation

- Organized crime in Afghanistan
- Organized crime in Albania
- Organized crime in Australia
- Organized crime in Brazil
- Organized crime in Bulgaria
- Organized crime in China
- Organized crime in France
- Organized crime in Greece
- Organized crime in India
- Organized crime in Ireland
- Organized crime in Italy
- Organized crime in Japan
- Organized crime in Kenya
- Organized crime in Kyrgyzstan
- Organized crime in Lebanon
- Organized crime in the Netherlands
- Organized crime in Nigeria
- Organized crime in Pakistan
- Organized crime in Quebec (province of Canada)
- Organized crime in Russia
- Organized crime in South Korea
- Organized crime in Sweden
- Organized crime in Turkey
- Organized crime in Ukraine
- Organized crime in the United Kingdom
- Organized crime in the United States
- Organized crime in Vietnam

## External links

 Wikiquote has quotations related to: *Organized crime*

Wikimedia Commons has media related to *Organized crime*.

- Mob Life: Gangster Kings of Crime[30] — slideshow by *Life* magazine
- UNODC - United Nations Office on Drugs and Crime[31] — sub-section dealing with organised crime worldwide
- "Organized Crime"[32] — Oxford Bibliographies Online: Criminology

# Appendix

## References

[1] //en.wikipedia.org/w/index.php?title=Template:Criminology_and_penology&action=edit
[2] Macionis, Gerber, John, Linda (2010). Sociology 7th Canadian Ed. Toronto, Ontario: Pearson Canada Inc. p. 206.
[3] Gambetta, D. (1996). The Sicilian Mafia: the business of private protection. Harvard University Press.
[4] Varese, F. (2001). The Russian Mafia: private protection in a new market economy. Oxford University Press.
[5] Wang, Peng (2017). The Chinese Mafia: Organized Crime, Corruption, and Extra-Legal Protection. Oxford: Oxford University Press.
[6] Chu, Y. K. (2002). The triads as business. Routledge.
[7] Hill, P. B. (2003). The Japanese mafia: Yakuza, law, and the state. Oxford University Press
[8] Tilly, Charles. 1985. "State Formation as Organized Crime". In Evans, Peter, Dietrich Rueschemeyer, and Theda Skocpol, eds.: *Bringing the State Back In*. Cambridge: Cambridge University Press.
[9] Interview with Panos Kostakos (2012) Is Oil Smuggling and Organized Crime the Cause of Greece's Economic Crisis http://oilprice.com/Energy/Energy-General/Greece-Oil-Smuggling-Helps-Define-the-Parliamentary-Mafiocracy.html? (by Jen Alic)
[10] Dominic Casciani, BBC News Home Affairs correspondent: 28 July 2011 *Criminal assets worth record £1bn seized by police* https://www.bbc.co.uk/news/uk-14318162
[11] Miller, W.B. 1992 (Revised from 1982). Crime by Youth Gangs and Groups in the United States. Washington, DC: U.S. Department of Justice, Office of JusticePrograms, Office of Juvenile Justice and Delinquency Prevention.
[12] Angus Martyn, The Right of Self-Defence under International Law-the Response to the Terrorist Attacks of 11 September http://www.aph.gov.au/library/Pubs/CIB/2001-02/02cib08.htm , Australian Law and Bills Digest Group, Parliament of Australia Web Site, 12 February 2002.
[13] Thalif Deen. POLITICS: U.N. Member States Struggle to Define Terrorism http://ipsnews.net/news.asp?idnews=29633 , Inter Press Service, 25 July 2005.
[14] Fighting financial crime http://www.fsa.gov.uk/about/what/financial_crime, FSA.gov.uk, Retrieved November 7, 2013
[15] Clarke, Richard A. *Cyber War*, HarperCollins (2010)
[16] "Cyberwar: War in the Fifth Domain" http://www.economist.com/node/16481504?story_id=16481504&source=features_box1 *Economist*, July 1, 2010
[17] Lynn, William J. III. "Defending a New Domain: The Pentagon's Cyberstrategy" http://www.foreignaffairs.com/articles/66552/william-j-lynn-iii/defending-a-new-domain, *Foreign Affairs*, September/October 2010, pp. 97-108
[18]
[19] "Malware Hits Computerized Industrial Equipment" http://bits.blogs.nytimes.com/2010/09/24/malware-hits-computerized-industrial-equipment/ *New York Times*, September 24, 2010
[20] African corruption 'on the wane' http://news.bbc.co.uk/1/hi/business/6288400.stm, 10 July 2007, BBC News
[21] Trafficking in Persons: Global Patterns http://www.unodc.org/pdf/traffickinginpersons_report_2006ver2.pdf, the 2006 UNODC Anti-Human Trafficking Unit report
[22] Sex Slaves: Estimating Numbers https://www.pbs.org/wgbh/pages/frontline/slaves/etc/stats.html, Public Broadcasting System "Frontline" fact site.
[23] Paul Lunde, *Organized Crime*, 2004.
[24] Sullivan, Robert, ed. *Mobsters and Gangsters: Organized Crime in America, from Al Capone to Tony Soprano*. New York: Life Books, 2002.
[25] Macintyre, Ben (1997). *The Napoleon of Crime: The Life and Times of Adam Worth*, Master Thief. Delta. p. 6-7.

[26] Robb, Brian J. *A Brief History of Gangsters*. Running Press (January 6, 2015). Chapter 1: Lawlessness in the Old West.
[27] Turner, Erin H. *Badasses of the Old West: True Stories of Outlaws on the Edge*. TwoDot; First edition (September 18, 2009). p. 132.
[28] Alexander, Bob. *Bad Company and Burnt Powder: Justice and Injustice in the Old Southwest (Frances B. Vick Series)*. University of North Texas Press; 1st edition (July 10, 2014). p. 259-261.
[29] http://laws-lois.justice.gc.ca/eng/acts/C-46/page-236.html#docCont
[30] https://web.archive.org/web/20110210040158/http://www.life.com/image/first/in-gallery/37642/mob-life-gangster-kings-of-crime
[31] http://www.unodc.org/unodc/en/organized-crime/index.html
[32] http://oxfordbibliographiesonline.com/display/id/obo-9780195396607-0021

# Article Sources and Contributors

The sources listed for each article provide more detailed licensing information including the copyright status, the copyright owner, and the license conditions.

**Organized crime**  *Source*: https://en.wikipedia.org/w/index.php?oldid=863002243  *License*: Creative Commons Attribution-Share Alike 3.0  *Contributors*:  4thaugust1932, 4twenty42o, Albany NY, Alexb102072, Amortias, Andy M. Wang, Anna Frodesiak, Antiqueight, Asdklf;, BDD, BFlatley, Babitaarora, Baking Soda, Bender235, Bennyben1398, Blnarloch, BreakfastJr, Buster7, Chris the speller, Clarinetguy097, Clean Copy, ClueBot NG, Coderzombie, Cohobbitation, Coltsfan, Countzander, Crystallizedcarbon, CsDix, Cyberbot II, DemocraticLuntz, Dewritech, Discospinster, DocWatson42, Dunnesite52,0, DuppaBuppa, Edward, Epicgenius, Erier2003, Ezavalas, First Light, Fivult, Fugitron, FungusFromYuggoth, FutureTrillionaire, George100, George8211, Godzilladude123, GregKaye, Greyjoy, Guillaumefg, Guitarmike612, GünniX, Harayz, Headbomb, Helmetdog, Hendrick 99, Himynameisdarthvader, Hmainsbot1, Holdek, Home Lander, Howicus, I dream of horses, I.C. Rivers, Insane.kismanO, InterestingCircle, Irfan Malik don, Itsalleasy, J 1982, Jack Armweak, Jack Greenmaven, JaconaFrere, Jarble, JesseRafe, Jessicapierce, Jim1138, JoeSperrazza, John of Reading, Johnappleseed82, Johnbod, Johngot, K6ka, KBH96, KGirlTrucker81, Keith D, Kku, Krakkos, Largoplazo, Legis, LieutenantLatvia, LilHelpa, Loganpedersen37, Lotje, Lunaraurora, Luuk de Brouwer, MadGuy7023, Madreterra, Mafia-research, Magioladitis, Mandruss, Marcocapelle, Materialscientist, MattW93, Merlinsorca, Modernist, Mohamed CJ, Mr Serjeant Buzfuz, Natemup, NeilN, Neutrality, NewEnglandYankee, Nick Moyes, Orduin, Orgcrim, Owqifoeiwdwe, Pbrower2a, Pencilsharper, PhantomTech, Prhartcom, Raymond1922A, Regulov, Rich Janis, Rjwilmsi, Rrburke, SFK2, Samantha Ireland, Sardanaphalus, SchreiberBike, Shotwth, Sluzzelin, Smashbackdoors, Squiver, Stoker91, SuperbowserX, Superspectre227, TAnthony, TTTAssasinator, TaylorPrice, The Rattler, TheClutchHand, Theinstantmatrix, Thetrigga, Timedrapery, Tjg110, Tobby72, Tonygibbs1981, ToonLucas22, Toughpigs, Tramadul, Twinsay, Usernamekiran, Vaselineeeeeeee, WEIRDO.Nerd, Wavedvales737,347, WayKurat, Weldspeale, Welsh, Widr, XXzoonamiXX, XxFire ReaperxX, Yamaguchi先生, Yourstil, 토마토양매추, 160 anonymous edits .................................................................................................................. 1

# Image Sources, Licenses and Contributors

The sources listed for each image provide more detailed licensing information including the copyright status, the copyright owner, and the license conditions.

**Image** *Source:* https://en.wikipedia.org/w/index.php?title=File:Pentonvilleiso19.jpg *License:* Public Domain *Contributors:* Joshua Jebb or employee 1
**Figure 1** *Source:* https://en.wikipedia.org/w/index.php?title=File:Christopher_Coke.jpg *License:* Public Domain *Contributors:* U.S. Marshal's Service ............................................................................................................................................ 4
**Figure 2** *Source:* https://en.wikipedia.org/w/index.php?title=File:Mexican_drug_cartels_2008.jpg *License:* Public Domain *Contributors:* US CONGRESS, COMMITTEE ON FOREIGN RELATIONS ............................................................................... 15
**Figure 3** *Source:* https://en.wikipedia.org/w/index.php?title=File:Marukin_at_Sanja_Matsuri_2.jpg *License:* Creative Commons Attribution 2.0 *Contributors:* Jorge from Tokyo, Japan ........................................................................................................ 18
**Image** *Source:* https://en.wikipedia.org/w/index.php?title=File:Wikiquote-logo.svg *License:* Public Domain *Contributors:* Rei-artur .......... 29
**Image** *Source:* https://en.wikipedia.org/w/index.php?title=File:Commons-logo.svg *License:* logo *Contributors:* Anomie, Callanecc, CambridgeBay-Weather, Jo-Jo Eumerus, RHaworth .................................................................................................................... 30

# License

Creative Commons Attribution-Share Alike 3.0
//creativecommons.org/licenses/by-sa/3.0/

# Index

Adam Worth, 17
Advance-fee fraud, 12
Adware, 13
Africa, 17
Agreement on Trade-Related Aspects of Intellectual Property Rights, 12
Albanian mafia, 29
Al Capone, 31
Al-Qaeda, 9, 27
American Mafia, 23
Animal Liberation Front, 9
Antiquities, 7
Arms trafficking, 7, 9
Army of God (USA), 9
Arson, 9
Article 41-bis prison regime, 28
Art theft, 7
Aryan Brotherhood, 27
Asia, 17
Assassination, 7
Assault, 8

Bandit, 17
Banditry, 17
Bandwidth (computing), 23
Bank robbery, 7
Bank Secrecy Act, 28
Barrio Azteca, 23
BBC News, 31
Belgium, 16
Bid rigging, 7
Black Liberation Army, 9
Blackmailing, 7
Bombing, 7
Bookmaking, 7
Boryokudan, 6
Boston, 23
Bribery, 7, 14
Bulgarian mafia, 29
Bureau of Alcohol, Tobacco, Firearms, and Explosives, 24
Business entity, 14
Business oligarch, 2
Butch Cassidys Wild Bunch, 18

Cali cartel, 27
Camorra, 23
Car theft, 7
Castellamarese war, 23
Charbonneau Commission, 29
Chicago Police, 24
Child, 15
Christopher Coke, 4
Civilians, 9
Civil procedure, 12
Civil society, 23
Cochise County Cowboys, 18
Code of silence, 9
Coercion, 9
Coercive, 8
Commons:Category:Organized crime, 30
Communist Bloc, 23
Computer crime, 13
Computer worm, 13
Confidence trick, 7
Continuing Criminal Enterprise, 28
Contract killing, 7
Controversy over terms, 13
Convention against Transnational Organized Crime, 16, 21, 28
Conventional warfare, 13
Copyright, 12
Copyright infringement, 7
Corporate liability, 14
Corporation, 14
Corsican mafia, 6
Counterfeiting, 7, 14
Coyotaje, 16
Crime in Brazil, 29
Crimes against humanity, 9
Criminal, 12
Criminal Assets Bureau, 28
Criminal Code (Canada), 28
Criminals, 1
Criminology, 1
Cronyism, 14
Cyber Command, 13
Cybercop, 23
Cyber spying, 13

Debt bondage, 16
Denial-of-service attack, 23
Derivative work, 12
Diego Gambetta, 1, 31
Diplomatic Security Service, 24
Dissolution of the Soviet Union, 23
Donald Cressey, 18
Drug cartel, 2, 15
Drug Enforcement Administration, 24
Drug trafficking, 7, 14

Earth Liberation Front, 9
Eastern Europe, 23
E-commerce, 23
Economic Espionage Act of 1996, 7
Electoral fraud, 7
Email fraud, 12
Embezzlement, 7, 14
Employment, 2
Employment scams, 12
Espionage, 13
Ethnic succession theory, 27
Exclusive right, 12
Extortion, 9, 13, 14, 23

Failed state, 1
Federal Bureau of Investigation, 16, 23
Federal Security Service (Russia), 24
Federal Wire Act, 28
Fence (criminal), 7
Financial Action Task Force on Money Laundering, 10
Financial crimes, 1
Forced prostitution, 15
Fraud, 12, 13
Fraud Enforcement and Recovery Act of 2009, 28

Gang, 1
Gangs in the United Kingdom, 29
Gennaro Angiulo, 23
German Nazi Party, 9
Germany, 16
Golden Crescent, 15
Golden Triangle (Southeast Asia), 15
Goths, 17
Government, 14
Graft (politics), 14
Greek mafia, 29

Hacker (computer security), 7
Highwayman, 17
History of Organized Crime in Saigon, 29
Hit man, 8
Hobbs Act, 28
House of cards, 3

Human trafficking, 14, 15

Identity document forgery, 7
Identity theft, 7, 23
Illegal drug trade, 16
Illegal drug trade in Colombia, 6
Illegal gambling, 7
Illegal taxicab operation, 7
Immigration and Customs Enforcement, 24
Indian subcontinent, 17
Informant, 23
Information warfare, 13
In international law, 9
Insider trading, 14
Institutionalization, 1
Insurance fraud, 7
International Organization for Migration, 16
Internet, 12, 23
Inter Press Service, 31
Irish Mob, 23, 27, 29
Irish Republican Army, 9
Islamic State of Iraq and the Levant, 28
Israel, 16
Italian-American Mafia, 27
Italy, 16, 17

Jamaican posses, 6
Japan, 16, 17
Jewish-American organized crime, 23

Kidnapping, 7
Kkangpae, 6, 29
Kleptocracy, 15
Kurdistan Workers Party, 9

Lashkar e Toiba, 9
Law, 9
Lebanese mafia, 29
Life (magazine), 30
List of designated terrorist groups, 9
List of law enforcement agencies, 23
Loan sharks, 16
Los Angeles Police Department, 24
Los Zetas, 27

Maharashtra Control of Organised Crime Act, 28
Malware, 13
Mara Salvatrucha, 23
Massachusetts State Police, 24
May 19th Communist Organization, 9
Medellin cartel, 27
Mexican Drug War, 2
Meyer Lansky, 19
Milieu (organized crime in France), 29
Military personnel, 9

38

Money, 1
Money laundering, 7, 14
Money Laundering Control Act, 28
Money transmitter, 10
Mongols, 17
Mungiki, 29
Murder, 8

Natural person, 14
Ndrangheta, 23
Nepotism, 14
Netherlands, 16
Neutrality (international relations), 9
New Jersey State Police, 24
New York City Police Department, 24
New York State Police, 24
Non-combatant, 9
Norsemen, 17
Nuremberg Trials, 9

Offshore bank, 11
Old West, 18
Opium production in Afghanistan, 29
Organised crime in India, 23
Organised crime in Pakistan, 29
Organized crime, **1**, 29
Organized Crime Control Act, 2, 28
Organized crime in Australia, 29
Organized crime in China, 29
Organized crime in India, 29
Organized crime in Italy, 29
Organized crime in Nigeria, 6, 29
Organized crime in Sweden, 29
Organized crime in the United States, 29
Organ trafficking, 7
Outlaw motorcycle club, 23

Passport fraud, 7
Patriarca crime family, 23
Patronage, 14
Pennsylvania State Police, 24
Penology, 1
Penose, 29
Philadelphia Police Department, 24
Phishing, 12
Pillaging, 17
Piracy, 17
Pirate, 17
Point shaving, 7
Police brutality, 14
Political corruption, 7, 14, 26
Political crime, 1
Political repression, 14
Polizia di Stato, 24
Power (social and political), 1
Price fixing, 7

Professor Moriarty, 17
Profit (economics), 1
Profit maximization, 20
Prostitution, 7, 15
Protection racket, 1, 9, 26
Protocol against the Smuggling of Migrants by Land, Sea and Air, 28
Protocol to Prevent, Suppress and Punish Trafficking in Persons, especially Women and Children, 28
Public Broadcasting System, 31
Pump and dump, 7

Racket (crime), 2
Racketeer Influenced and Corrupt Organizations Act, 9, 28
Revolutionary Armed Forces of Colombia, 9
Revolutions of 1989, 23
Robbery, 8
Robert K. Merton, 26
Romance scam, 12
Rootkit, 13
Royal Canadian Mounted Police, 24
Rule of law, 23
Russian Mafia, 23, 27, 29

Sabotage, 13
Sacra Corona Unita, 23
Satellite, 13
Secretary of Defense, 13
Securities fraud, 7
Seduction, 7
Serious Organised Crime and Police Act 2005, 28
Sexual assault, 9
Shoplifting, 7
Sicilian Mafia, 6, 8, 23, 27
Sicily, 27
Skimming (fraud), 7
Slavery, 16
Smuggling, 7
Snakehead (gang), 16
South Asia, 16
Spyware, 13
State crime, 1
Symbionese Liberation Army, 9

Taliban, 9, 27
Tax haven, 11
Tax shelter, 11
Template:Criminology and penology, 1
Template talk:Criminology and penology, 1
Terrorism, 1, 26
Thailand, 16
The Covenant, The Sword, and the Arm of the Lord, 9

The Order (white supremacist group), 9
The Pentagon, 13
Thief in law, 23
Thuggee, 17
Tijuana Cartel, 27
Title 21 of the United States Code, 28
Tong (organization), 23
Tony Soprano, 31
Trafficking in human beings, 7
Transnational organized crime, 1
Treason, 1
Triad (organized crime), 23
Triad society, 6
Trojan horse (computing), 13
Tulip Revolution, 29
Turkey, 16
Turkic peoples, 17
Turkish mafia, 29

Ukrainian mafia, 29
Unfree labor, 14
UNICEF, 16
United Freedom Front, 9
United Nations Office on Drugs and Crime, 16
United States, 2, 16
United States Border Patrol, 24
United States Coast Guard, 24
United States Department of Justice, 2
United States Marshals Service, 24
United States Patriot Act, 28
United States Postal Inspection Service, 24
United States Secret Service, 24
UNODC, 31
Unsupported attributions, 2
U.S. Customs and Border Protection, 24

Vandals, 17
Vicarious liability (criminal), 14
Victorian era, 17
Vulnerability (computing), 13

War crimes, 1
Washington, D.C., 24
Weather Underground, 9
White-collar crime, 1, 26
Whitey Bulger, 23
Wikipedia:Citation needed, 9, 12
William J. Lynn, 13
Winter Hill Gang, 23
Woman, 15

Yakuza, 6, 8, 18, 23
Yakuza (organized crime in Japan), 29

www.ingramcontent.com/pod-product-compliance
Lightning Source LLC
Chambersburg PA
CBHW051350040426
42453CB00007B/508